Countries

Kenya

by Christine Juarez

raintree

a Capstone company — publishers for children

Raintree is an imprint of Capstone Global Library Limited, a company incorporated in England and Wales having its registered office at 264 Banbury Road, Oxford, OX2 7DY – Registered company number: 6695582

www.raintree.co.uk
myorders@raintree.co.uk

Edited by Erika L. Shores
Designed by Bobbie Nuytten
Picture research by Tracy Cummins
Production by Laura Manthe

Printed in China
ISBN 978 1 4747 1981 0
20 19 18 17 16
10 9 8 7 6 5 4 3 2 1

British Library Cataloguing in Publication Data
A full catalogue record for this book is available from the British Library.

Photo Credits
Flickr: Mark Skipper, 13; Getty Images: Nigel Pavitt, 11; Newscom: DANIEL IRUNGU/EPA, 15, Sergio Pitamitz/Robert Harding, 19, Stephen Morrison/EPA, 17; Photos.com: Stockbyte, 22; Shutterstock: Andrzej Kubik, 1, Itinerant Lens, 9, Ivsanmas, 4, KA Photography KEVM111, 21, Natalia Pushchina, 5, Ohmega1982, back cover (globe), Oleg_Mit, 22, Paul Banton, cover, PHOTOCREO/Michal Bednarek, 7, sahua d, cover, 1 (design element)

We would like to thank Gail Saunders-Smith, Ph.D., for her invaluable help in the preparation of this book.

Note to Parents and Teachers

The Countries series supports learning related to people, places, and culture. This book describes and illustrates Kenya. The images support early readers in understanding the text. The repetition of words and phrases helps early readers learn new words. This book also introduces early readers to subject-specific vocabulary, which is defined in the Glossary section. Early readers may need assistance to read some words and to use the Contents, Glossary, Read more, Websites and Index sections of the book.

Contents

Where is Kenya?

Kenya is a country in East Africa. It is just over twice the size of the United Kingdom. Kenya's capital is Nairobi.

KENYA

★*Nairobi*

Landforms

Kenya has many landforms. Beaches line the coast of the Indian Ocean. Savannahs and the Chalbi Desert are north of the coasts. Mountains are in the west.

Animals

In Kenya, lions and cheetahs

chase antelope across savannahs.

Hippos cool themselves in

muddy rivers. Elephants, zebras

and giraffes also roam Kenya.

Language and population

Kenya has 44 million people.

Most Kenyans live in the countryside.

Kenyans speak Kiswahili or English.

Other languages are spoken by

different groups of indigenous people.

Food

Corn is the main food in Kenya.

Ugali is a common dish. It is

made of corn flour and water.

It becomes a dough that Kenyans

eat with vegetables or meat.

13

Celebrations

Kenyans celebrate Jamhuri Day
on 12 December. It marks the day
Kenya became its own country.
People enjoy large meals,
dancing and parades.

Where people work

Many Kenyans are farmers. Coffee beans and tea grow on large farms. Farmers sell these crops for money. On smaller farms, people grow corn to feed their families.

Transportation

Many Kenyans walk from place to place. In cities, people might take buses or taxis. People travel between large cities by train.

Famous sight

People come from all over the world to see Kenya's wildlife. Visitors to Nairobi National Park look for lions, cheetahs, rhinos, giraffes and zebras.

Country facts

Name: Republic of Kenya

Capital: Nairobi

Population: 44,037,656 (July 2013 estimate)

Size: 582,649 square kilometres (224,962 square miles)

Languages: English, Kiswahili and many indigenous languages

Main crops: tea, coffee, corn, wheat, sugar cane, fruit

Money: Kenyan shilling

Kenya's flag

Glossary

antelope animal that looks like a large deer and runs very fast

capital city in a country where the government is based

celebrate do something fun on a special day

coast land near an ocean or sea

crop plant farmers grow in large amounts; usually for food

desert dry area with little rain

indigenous to do with people who traditionally live in a certain place

landform natural feature of the land

language words used in a particular country or by a particular group of people

national park land set aside by a country in order to protect the plant and animal life

savannah flat, grassy area of land with few or no trees

taxi car with a driver whom you pay to take you where you want to go

Read more

Cultural Traditions in Kenya (Cultural Traditions in My World), Kylie Burns (Crabtree Publishing Company, 2015)

Kenya (Journey Through), Liz Gogerly (Franklin Watts, 2016)

Websites

ngkids.co.uk/places/country-fact-file-kenya
Learn about Kenya's culture, government, history and more.

www.timeforkids.com/destination/kenya
Go on a journey around the world and discover fun facts about Kenya.

Index